Caterpillar Face

A Collection of Poetry by Uxia Rose

FIRST EDITION

ISBN: 979-8-9927136-0-2

Cover photo by Alex Zammarieh

For you, Caterpillar Face

Caterpillar Face

Before

down hallways and sidewalks

it's always the same

through windows and water

she's always searching

for a glimpse of her face

Caterpillar Face

The Traveler

I pack two bags to leave a place
of disconnected disconnections
which make me numb and deaf.

To head for a place of uncertainty
where glass shatters down my back
and I sit with a half dead dolphin.

A place where I must feel my pain
because I can't read the label on the bottle of pills
and the nearest doctor they call witch.

A place of real dangers
like a tropical plantation
too far for anyone to hear me scream.

A place of insulting honesty
where a man lives with a plastic chair
and sex is done in the streets.

A place of strange mysteries
that make leeches crawl on land
and real men slice the skin under their tongues.

A place that redefines cleanliness
as I wear my underpants full of sand
and little bits of flesh under my fingernails.

A place that opens me wide
to insert cows eating plastic
and the taste of turtle.

A place that makes me free
to get swept out to sea in a current
or die in a room with a bucket.

A place that makes me guilty
because you've never put fake butter on fake crackers
or sung to worms in a cave.

A place that disorients me
because my bed is full of bugs
and I am in the middle of an ocean.

A place that makes me listen
since I'm searching for sharks in winter while it's hot
and sitting in a car full of strangers.

A place I've become addicted to
because I love to rip the skin from between my toes
and sleep with a parasitic cat.

This is the place that I travel to,
the only place that I know.
This is the reason I can't stay
But, also, the reason I must go.

Caterpillar Face

It's hard to eat when there are rocks in your mouth.

They taste of being six years old. You'll choke or die first.

You'll think of that later.

You're distracted by the caterpillars crawling on your face.

They tickle you
but there are sea creatures inside not batteries: you can't
laugh.

Except when you remember a man reaching for the pet
spider that resides on your nipple.

He can't have it, it's always yours.

This is your cage-
earth's mirror, a nightmare that wakes and dreams.

The caterpillars are still crawling.

You match them with blue jeans but a face will always be a
peculiar place for a caterpillar.

Human

Thieves like vultures
found me
chasing my own tail un-bit,
their bite.
Still, they devour deeper
to destroy the mesmeric fact but
ignorance and pride already
hid the bestowal, the precious possession
eternally un-swallowed
somewhere far and ill-lit
so concealed as to be named lost
where all is unfound
then forgotten
by the hoarder and the hopeful.
Now left behind
I become the creature that can die.

Unconsciously Awake

When stillness without
I find feeling within.

Muscle moves
without a mind.

A world expands
inward then outward.

The path is given
but not taken.

Dharma is a secret
eight years old.

Wonderful/Terrible

On Sundays and
before breakfast
after kissing
and between stop signs
I think about

Ziplock bags
spinach
heroin
vaccines
Michael Jackson
operations
paper straws
breakups
fluoride
running
euthanasia
thorns
growing old
Santa Claus
forest fires
water shoes
rats
internet
and zoos

because maybe
if I can understand one of these things
then I won't be ashamed of dancing
and the nighttime
and desire

A LITTLE THING

the difference between water at 32 and 33 degrees

unwilling wrists in hands closed tightly

the early frost that kills the crop

human thrown against a wall

air bubbles in drying clay

brain unable to process

an ember escaping the fire

perceptions in flashes instead of scenes

rancid meat consumed

huge hands stealing

a cigarette near the gas pump

figure appearing, disappearing

bleach instead of water

breath, the only sound left

sleeping while driving

red, blood red eyes blind

one misoprostol tablet

unconscious dead smile, a ghost

a room with lead paint

a repugnant cloud, a face contorted

a tiny pair of viper fangs

clothes lose value

breathing under water

hair disrupted; skin disturbed

slits across your wrists

fingers linger on a belly

the edge of a cliff, falling

down. down. down.

a rutting bison too close

under, through, between, inside

an artery blocked

a soul floats away

bullet in the brain

body left deserted

a death cap instead of a puffball

body left behind

it's a little mistake but you die

In the Pitch Black

you never say
thank you
or please or
you're welcome.
Money is only paper.
Love is never true.
Food has no taste.
Right and wrong
sound the same.
You exist there alone,
you left your children behind.
Regardless of your eyes
in the darkness you're blind.

Handprints

there are handprints upon my skin
left by a vile touch
their impression is a constant torment
a brand that never stops burning

the handprints taught me hate
hate for the body that wears them

I scrub them
they never fade
no matter the soap
or how raw I rub them
I cover them
I still feel them
I place more handprints on top
I can't bury them

left with no choice
I cut the flesh away that bears them

with skin hanging and blood dripping
I realize

the handprints are inside

Starving

When did my bones become so beautiful?

Like branches on a tree poking.

I want you to see them.

See me,

see how beautiful we are.

Watch as I pull back the skin

that's obstructing your view.

I was hoping

if I show you

the one way

I'm perfect

maybe you'll love me.

Lonely Space

Anywhere I can be is a desolate place to float.

Even gravity will not hold me.

This bleak body depresses into a black hole

unable to consume

even the hopeful, distant light of stars.

I am surrounded by comfortless, icy ether

that darkens into the dreary night where I exist.

Its endless nature maddens me.

Time has forsaken me here,
and so have you.

Still

Your feet, they wander,
and your tongue slips.
You burn me and watch,
abandon me without a thought.
A subtle torture, my constant drought.
You purposefully forget,
put me down and tell me lies.
It's so easy to do
when you know
I still love you.

Black Tongue

grows while you're sleeping.
Terrifying it tastes
and the swallowing burns
the little bits left fighting.
Resistance to quell but
vigorously you tire
as a weakened house.
Home is the bed you fall onto.
Unknown rest remains unknown.
You are weeping.

Soon

Climb into my arms.
Let me hold you
and tell you
all you've been wanting to hear.

[everything will be all right]

Soon
all this pain will make you beautiful.

Washroom Relationships

I look into the toilet, my true mirror

which shows me what a waste I am

I offer my contents in exchange for its lies

an arrangement we've made

after

I roll myself into a fetal ball

the cold floor holds me adamantly

my fingers trace it

as my tears collect in the grout lines

The Mountain

Every day the sky told the mountain how beautiful she was.
Every day the mountain did not understand.
She had never seen her reflection in the ocean,
this mountain was surrounded by land.

Every day wind and water eroded the mountain away.
Every day the mountain shrank farther into the ground.
If only she knew how beautiful she was, she
wouldn't have disappeared, never to be found.

Like Alice

A rabbit hole dropped me
slashing and twisting onto a picnic table,

> appearing and disappearing on a picnic table.
> My body violently shrank and stretched.

My mind strangely shrank and stretched.
I no longer understood time.

> I no longer understand time.
> The truth kissed me on the lips.

A mad stranger kissed me on the lips.
A cloud of smoke appears a caterpillar.

> A cat, a queen, Absolem the caterpillar.
> An evil queen and her castle inside of my heart.

Her head hangs on my wall, next to my heart.
A rabbit hole dropped me.

I Must Thank You

you were the first pernicious vice to save me.
a deeper earth wisdom pervaded your toxic sharing.
how could you sit with such medicine
and not allow yourself to heal?
even medicine
can't heal
a person who does not want to get better.
even the earth couldn't stop me from hurting myself
but she did teach me how sick I was
and showed me I could heal myself.

Airline Emergency

When the masks dropped down
        I jumped up, I stumbled around
                I ripped masks from passenger's hands
        I forced them onto their faces.
                All along
                                I was suffocating.

The flight attendant said
'Ma'am, take your seat.'
'Ma'am, please sit down!' still
        I continued until I collapsed.
        I never wanted to wake up but
the plane never crashed.

This Time

You want to ask the people around you for help
but it's like wanting a drink of water from the ocean
and making the sentence is like
making a crossword without any vowels
but you're desperate enough, starving enough that
you reach your neck right over the barbed wire fence.
Admitting that you are not what you seem hurts
like the whole class pointing and laughing but
you aren't embarrassed because no one is listening
as if you whispered it in the Star Mountains
and then you are alone all over again
just like before and like yesterday and tomorrow
but you aren't allowed to die yet, even if you want to
because you are only a seedling in spring.
Still, you walk out into the water to try.
Your murky reflection stops your remains.
It whispers, save yourself this time.

100 Days

one, two
give me something else to do

three, four
one day more

five, six
still no fix

seven, eight
better late

nine, ten
another day, count again

eleven, twelve, thirteen
fourteen, fifteen, sixteen
life becomes a smoke screen

seventeen, eighteen, nineteen, twenty
my body is starving but I'm eating plenty

twenty-one through twenty-five
do not give up, stay alive

twenty-six
still no fix

twenty-seven
long for heaven

twenty-eight and nine and thirty
my mouth is clean but I feel dirty

thirty-one
still no fun

thirty-two to forty-two
I hate you

forty-three
lonely

forty-four
please no more

forty-five, forty-six, forty-seven, forty-eight
clean slate

forty-nine to sixty-nine
cry every day but we're fine

seventy
I want to quit endlessly

seventy-one to seventy-three
counting to be free

seventy-four
twenty-six days more

seventy-five to eighty-two
do not fall through

eighty-three
lay by the sea

eighty-four, eighty-five, eighty-six
know your tricks

eighty-seven to ninety-four
I don't want to count anymore

ninety-five to ninety-eight
almost time to celebrate

ninety-nine
I caress the finish line

one hundred

Everything

Mosquito nets don't protect you from the strange men who quietly slip into your room at night.

A night where you never close your eyes until you're hidden behind a child's body.

A body you want to help. Despite your own safety, you say yes.

Yes, to a taxi driver in a blue truck who feeds you fish and chocolate cake for breakfast.

The breakfast you hope is poisonous. You hope for anything to end your misery.

Your miserable self that doesn't feel anything anymore.

Until a strange man slips into your room.

Afraid, you feel everything.

Lonely and her Lover

as i wait to be
maybe only time can heal.
time is a dripping sink
i will not understand.

clouds like rain
but never rain.

comfort never asks
uncomfortable questions.
neither do you.

bizarre and twisted
because you're numb to good.
i let you touch me
so i'll be numb too.

you make it easy and smooth until
everything becomes blurry.

i locked the door.
still, you came in.

i can't put you out,
can't be
rood. rude. rood. rude.

wanting to be special
meant to be bland.

i wish you would
just hold my hand.

no one can help me
but myself
but I'm tired

oh, i really want help

The Sale

I sold my body to numb the pain.
Instead of crying, I whisper your name.

I look in your eyes, I look at my shame.
I look in the mirror, I look the same.
I look again; my body is stained.

I try to wash myself down the drain.
Still, somehow, I always remain.

Pink flesh against a blade...
Instead, another sale is made.

Night People

A secret lover in the night.
It isn't cold but I hold him tight.

My dreams are better this way.

No matter, he won't stay all night.
He's always gone with the light.

Now I've begun to hate the day.

Masterpiece

My torn body laid in torn pieces across the floor.
It was hard not to step on it as you walked through the door.

At first, in horror, you turned away.
You turned to leave me there where I lay.

But instead, you paused.
In the gore, something you saw.

Skin, bone, blood, long brown hair
nearly a corpse, still you saw it there.

Straight to work, you knelt on the ground.
A pile of supplies the artist had found.

The pieces were slimy and slipped as you picked them up.
Your awkward long fingers, a gentle touch.

You licked the back of the pieces of skin
grabbed a piece of my body, stuck it back in.

You put the pieces back in a different place than before.
When you were done, I did not look the same anymore.

Slowly you healed me; I became alert.
I cried the whole time; the processes hurt.

I looked down at my body as I started to move.
I did not want to admit I could be improved

but you were right; the artist knew.
I am more beautiful than before; I see it too.

I am forever grateful that you saw me here
but I haven't been fooled, your motives were clear.

When you saw me in pieces there on the floor
you thought no one should see my mess anymore.

You made me into something nicer to see.
You didn't care for my pain or even notice me.

Now you kiss me, and cry. You don't want me to leave.
You're losing your masterpiece, of course you must grieve.

You say, "I love you," but you love the art that you made.
I say I love you too, my love for your work, a fair trade.

Waves

You are a wave, on a wave, on a wave.
They carried us
tossed us together with salt
I still taste.

Waves carried us together
waves carried us apart
but I never forgot
and I'll never forget.

Sometimes I sit with them still.
I watch their rage.
They crash in anger over and over.
I feel my own fury.

I imagine the ocean watching
and a terrible storm
in outrage.
Waves thrashing.

I imagine vengeance.
The waves reaching out to
drag him down
into their darkness.

I hope they reached out for you too.
Carried you away
somewhere safe.
Somewhere you are smiling.

If I were the waves
I would wash away the whole world
for you.
In fairness.

Instead
I sit in the edges of the water
making you promises
to counterbalance evil.

So many foreign shores
I sat
and still sit
but the waves do not take.

I will not waste
what's left wandering
unsettled
by the sea.

I will offer
what is here.
What is alive.
What is aimless.

I will visit you
in the sea
along the way
and tell you stories.

I wave to you from the shore.
I blow kisses
and say prayers.
You wave back.

All this time
gone by
I will not
let you go.

Thank you
for your life
and your waves.
They are beautiful.

In loving memory of Elly Warren

In Plain Sight

You are looking for me again.
You won't see me under the secrets
that are out behind the shed and
on the corner of that old couch
in that old, abandoned house
and in all those bushes
even though that is where I am.
You won't find me wasting away in memories
like the cat litter that smells
like pornography and the
sweet pain of my teeth growing in
and the first time I read
What To Expect When You're Expecting.
I'm hiding.

Destruction Creates

Destruction is a moment,
the moment you make contact.

Creation is a lifetime,
the lifetime passing by.

I will always be recreating what you destroyed.
I will always be recreating what I destroyed.

Why do humans want to destroy everything they see?
Why did you think you could destroy me?

No one told you.
In the end

we destroy ourselves.

The Year I Learned to Make Sushi

The friend became friendless.

A free woman became a slave.

A lover was left for longing.

I lost everything I ever gave.

The Traveler Returns

we transform when we're sleeping.
under the guise of wakefulness
imagination is reality.
only the empty mind can integrate.
a busy mind makes madness
in the simple man.
hindsight understands
pandemonium
when the past is present.
unprocessed sensations
make fools.
a fool never lived when
they die.

Lasting

I hold obsolete ideas in my small hands.
I carry cold lifeless bodies on my back.
I paint my lips with stale blood from my pockets.
I follow ten deranged toes through and between time.
I wear ancient lips that no longer speak or belong to me.
I grow empty while full of fading shadows.
I tire from tugging stagnant air through poisoned lungs.
I loose critical concepts through invisible cracks.

I lie, lie, lie then lie again.

I reach for the silence, perhaps it will be quiet then.

Jungle Nexus

A clammy presence caresses my skin.

It sings me a barbaric song until I close my eyes.

We are eternally present; we are part of each other.

I breathe life into myself as I exist in sensations.

I am overwhelmed as I disappear into nothingness.

There I find something more than myself-
a forest with roots deep within.

I taste heat and hear birds dancing.

I see the secrets trees carry to the sky and I smell the
animals laughing.

I stay as long as I can until

a distant voice calls me back.

Reflective Suicide Attempts

Inadequate.
Words always are.
For lifting
a child's body
off a table of food
where it collapsed
by its own hands.

And now
my hands
hold
what I do not understand.
The thing
I have been running from
but still
it finds me
in the darkest corners
of the Earth.

I can't escape it,
I can't escape myself.

The Most Beautiful Place

dazzles and delights
with perfection
a human never touched it

I smile and giggle
transfixed by the way

everything dies in peace
the earth and I sing in harmony
I never sang before

butterflies float and dance around me
the light wraps me in glory
birds never fly away
plants only grow

this place is paradise
but I am the same

I HAVE TO GET OUT OF HERE
I HAVE TO GET OUT OF HERE
I HAVE TO GET OUT OF HERE

Never Alone

There is a dark shadow in the room.
A breeze caresses you.
A putrid smell: vomit baking in the sheets
then mold and cockroaches.
Your belongings are simple.
You are paralyzed calling into the night.

A long, dark, lonely night
long after the sun enters the room
and a sickness not simple
here to teach you.
Here among the cockroaches.
Here between the sheets.

Hallucinations in the sheets.
Nightmares not at night.
People too far to care, they are cockroaches.
They slip in and out of the room
as ghosts do. They leave you.
Leaving you is simple.

Pain is simple.
Pain wraps you like a sheet.
Pain is inside of you.
Pain is an endless night.
Pain is this room.
Pain eats you like cockroaches.

Consider cockroaches.
Killing them isn't simple
but you may die in this room.
A Roman wrapped in sheets
on a day like night
where no one loves you.

In delirium you say thank you
for the cockroaches
and for the night.
And for the body simple
that endlessly, tirelessly fights for you in the sheets
to escape from the room.

In sheets and cockroaches
in a night made simple
in a room, you whisper to your body, I love you.

Two Babies

I left two babies crying in the dark.
It was raining
so loud on the metal roof
I could barely hear the thunder.

They were wet.
They were desperate.
They were terrified.

I was dry.
I was hurting.
I was bitter.

Their cries came through the chaos as the sun cuts the
clouds.

No one answered my cries for help.
So, I didn't answer theirs.

Meredith

I stopped being friendly

       making friends or
              acquaintances or
       lovers

no more saying goodbye
no more tears to cry

              until Meredith

       Meredith with friends
   and lovers and
acquaintances

Meredith always saying goodbye
       Meredith loving goodbye
              Meredith loving to cry

The Mask

My mother will never get the chance to meet me.
She's looking right at me, but she can't see me.

Because I'm behind a mask I've been wearing too long.
When I took it off, it ripped my skin, now my face is gone.

I don't want to pretend to be someone else anymore
but how can I be who I am without my face from before.

I'd have destroyed the mask if I knew what it would erase
except it's been too long, I'm too late, this mask is my face.

Violence is Contagious

Your violent ways brought me violent dreams.
Whether in the woods or at work or in bed
I think about killing, what does that mean?

My visions are graphic, the violence obscene.
I cut off your toes, testicles, and head.
Your violent ways brought me violent dreams.

I caught your violence, that's how it seems.
I drown you in a river, I rip you open in a shed.
I think about killing, what does that mean?

I want you to suffer, I want you to scream.
My once gentle hands are now bloody and red.
Your violent ways brought me violent dreams.

How can I hurt you? I plot, and I scheme.
How many ways can I make you dead?
I think about killing, what does that mean?

The violence you feel isn't the violence on screens.
It's a vile, vicious beast who must be fed.
Your violent ways brought me violent dreams.
I think about killing, what does that mean?

White Summer

A white summer
is worn fresh on your skin
like a dive into icy water.
It has no time or place.
The air is freshly made
as it changes your mind
like raw bacon hitting a hot pan.
In fact, everything changes.
Especially the people.
They forget.
Lashing out recklessly
they consume each other.

A white summer
found me running down a hallway
trying to cover my swollen breasts
as I escaped a snake
who only spoke poison.
Before that, a monster called liar
whose room I broke into and
forced onto its bed
to offer my servitude.
I never had so many lovers and
I never had so many friends.
Secrets were on every wall and
under the legs of every table and chair.

In a white summer
you either eat too much
or not enough.
Food isn't how you survive.
You live off your addiction.
Although, it may not be a drug.
It may just taste like saltwater
or be a room full of empty bottles.
It may be an Australian man you met on the internet
or filling a box with cherries and olives.
It may be 2 hours asleep, and 22 hours awake.
It may be a place named after a dessert.

Have you had a white summer?
Do you understand why I hide?
And why they wrote all those lies?
And what happened in that red shirt and
why I drank that milkshake?
And why the bears stayed away from me?

Sustained

the earth is my mother's mother's mother
mother was sacrificed at conception
her children curse her
she only knows love
mother gives, never gets
though her children make offerings
a fly will never fill the belly of a bear yet

mother fills my mouth with salmon berries
until my belly is full
and my lips dripping
but I never say thank you
as I confuse a blessing with a birthright

Walking Mind

I have more companions than I can keep.
I never mean the words I speak.

You hold my time between your hands
as I wait for you to change my plans.

My lips are softer than you'd think.
These ideas I carry make me sink.

I say hello to say goodbye.
How will we live as we wait to die?

Waiting

I close my eyes
but still, I see
the curve of your lips
the bone of your cheek

hands to the sky
I pray for guidance
let me hear you speak
I sit in silence

you withhold your flame
I withhold my touch
I offer the truth
it isn't much

impossibly I reach, then
reason burns my heart
alone I become lonely
distance pulls me apart

smoke clears my mind
I wake up and dream
I feel what I feel
do you like how I seem

when to hold on
when to let go
patiently wait
to finally know

Say Something

To my horror

you trapped me in silence.

I wandered around and

banged the walls.

My strikes were soundless,

my clamoring too.

But the words you never said

were so loud

they left me deaf.

Left Behind

Coming home
everything was exactly the same
except that everything was completely different.

The same people knew my name
but now none of them knew what it meant.

There was still a mouth on my face
but it no longer knew how to speak.

The traffic lights and stop signs still made streets safe
but now the roads were boring and predictable.

I had nothing just like before
but now they wanted what I didn't have.

My family loved me the same as always
but now I resented them for being the same as always.

Chocolate was still bitter like coffee
but I craved a three-layer cake.

Confused, I left and left and left and
I'll never stop leaving
until I have a reason to stay.

What You Never Say

I hide small words inside of my mouth.
They're hidden between my teeth and
under my tongue.

They reach for you.

I won't let them out.

Today

another day waiting to be wanted more than everything else.
Another day waiting to be thought of before yourself.

Since today's a new day, I ask you again.
Today's not the day, but if not today then when?

I keep waiting so you'll have me even though I can't have you
I won't leave you lonely, but I'll stay lonely for you.

Eventually we know we will go our separate ways
but it's easier to push away the future these days.

I won't leave first because I believe that you'll let me.
I won't say goodbye to the only person who gets me.

But goodbye is for tomorrow and not for today.
Today we're together so that's why we stay.

My Captor

I am my captor

I hide myself away in small dark places

behind doors that I lock

inside of rooms I have made

between walls I have built

all to keep me from the world I created

Hunched

The droop in my shoulders expose
my broken veins and wretched skin.
They cover the horrible things
that I've come to find.
My servitude to selfishness and
the way that I give myself pain.
I'm an undisciplined disciple of myself
afraid of her master
and of sharing my gifts.
I endlessly want
what isn't mine. I
play it safe, but I play that as risks.
Stay safe from my subtle judgements,
my pretty lies and
my delusional mind.
I'm incapable of appreciating you.
It's why I constantly escape.
You'll never be enough
for my abundance of inadequacies.
I'm a perfectionist
at living which
will never be.
I only disappoint myself repeatedly
until disappointment grows
into disgust
which eventually becomes the hate
hidden in my heart that I
pour onto others
to have less of for myself.
But I never do.
So, I blame myself for things I never did
like hurricanes and
a missing cousin
and the shape of my nose.
I hate myself more
until I must pretend to be
someone else- the person you have met.

You never knew me but
I wish that you did.
You may feel surprised
but I know you're not who you say either.
I've seen what your shoulders hide.

Solitude was Never Safe

you are not hurting me anymore

you cannot hurt me anymore

you cannot find me anymore

who is still hurting me
here in a room with only myself

Reckless

I've been dancing
undressed
for Death.
I dance until I
rub myself
dirty on the ground.
My stage name is
Fearless
as I flirt with ending.
I dance until I collapse.
Death finally looks at me
says
"Keep dancing
to die
a desperate coward
otherwise
I'll come find you
when you're brave."

Windows

sometimes I walk alone at night.
as I do, I like to look in people's windows.
I want to see if they are as lonely as I am.
if they didn't want me to see
they would have shut their curtains
but they are, so they didn't.

My Favorite Place

People often ask my favorite place.
One of those wonders?
That distant magic forest?
Some sparkling shore?
The snow on that mountain?
The sand on that floor?
But I never tell them,

it's with you.

Watcher Who Loves You

You won't hear a single sound from my sabbatical
even though it's crashing and crying.
An absolute racket,
remembering the secrets of children.
Nothing is more honest
than a fight over a peanut butter and jelly sandwich.
We're both crying.
It's strange and raw
but two years is long enough to be a rival.
The competition can only be won by a garden snail.
You never stood a chance.
As the brain empties into repetition,
will you find intellect or madness?
You can survive with either
if you can lay down and wear it like a revealing dress.
The dress will be ripped open.
Can you sew?
Your mother never taught you
because no one taught her how to survive without herself.
It's like drowning
without a body to choke on the water.
It's exhausting
because you never die.
You'd be surprised
how long you can last in this condition.
It's a naked truth
when you don't have time to put on anything other than a
human.
And are you creative?
Because you must be
White matter needs stories and beliefs
like the difference between a dog and a person
and how there are different types of bread.
You never knew
you never knew a thing until
it's chewed up and spit back into your face.
It's probably vegetables.
And how's your stomach?

Because you'll wear it 'till it's dry.
Your hands are holding
the future and it's crying as if you are dreadful.
It's all worth it
when you realize
you only need a pool noodle
to be a firefighter
and the ocean is in your living room
It's pure.
One of the last pure things.
Even that is vanishing
but until it's gone
enjoy
doing nothing else with another person
except existing.

It's Me Not You

you can't leave.
we must stay together
until you have
enough memories
to never forget me.
only then,
when you can't remember
a life where I don't exist
and suddenly you need me,
I can go.

Rift

in January I want to be far away
somewhere strange and new
where everything I have is in a bag
no one knows where I am or what I do

in February I want a home that does not move
I want to grow plants and babies
as I watch the seasons come and go
I celebrate holidays and I decorate for parties

in March I must leave
somewhere won't stop calling me
it keeps me up at night
as if part of me lives across the sea

in April I only want to rest
in a bed that I own, in a room that I own
a bed that is not lonely
somewhere safe in a place that I've known

in May I am wild
so that is where I'll be hiding
I'll eat dehydrated food and look for bears
I don't have a map, the earth is guiding

in June I want pets
and a job and a car
I go on long walks
but I never walk too far

July is like May
and August is like June
I want one thing
but a different thing soon

so, I borrow other people's babies
and grow plants on airplanes while I am away
I am tired of constantly leaving
but for some reason I cannot breathe if I stay

Sandcastles

I remember wasted paper cups
beside little conversations
and our chairs drawn close.

I remember the color red in
a room full of religion
with bald heads and wrapped robes.

I remember other people
and the odor of peeled oranges
all around our obverse gaze.

I remember our struggle to speak.
A strange circumstance for us.
We stole simple lies from each other's lips

but we both knew the truth the whole time.
I was your sandcastle, and you were mine.

Living with Strangers

roommates are like changing rooms
you show them your private parts
then you never see them again

Lovely

isn't it lovely
the way that the dishes are never done
and our clothes are always dirty

isn't it lovely
the way we always bicker
never saying how we feel

isn't it lovely
how we irritate in the same ways
and change too slowly

isn't it lovely
how none of those things matter
when I need you, you are always there

Poetry Teacher

God taught me poetry.
I was clanky and awkward
sitting in the front row of church.
He spoke to me of deer and breasts and lilies.
I did not understand a single word
but it was the most beautiful thing I ever heard.

God taught me poetry
when I was a long blade of grass
bent over by the wind
somewhere the horizon didn't exist.
In awe I wrote down everything I could see.
He whispered in my ear, 'Love, that's poetry.'

God taught me poetry
as I watched a shriveled shrunken corpse
still somehow alive and an infant alone
in the dirt, chewing on a screw
He told me pleasure is a lie.
We're just as beautiful when we weep and break and die.

God taught me poetry
while I bobbed in a docked canoe
compressed by an untouchable sky.
Universes reflected on the black water.
He laughed as I gawked at his simple expression.
'Imagine what you write when you really see heaven.'

Grown Up

I was born with caterpillars on my face.
This bloody body is the strangest place.

I was born naked for everyone to see.
Now I cover the most beautiful parts of me.

I was born with unimaginable dreams in my head.
Those dreams will die as soon as I am dead.

I was born with a thousand words in my mouth.
You'll never hear what they are as loud as I shout.

I was born far from alone.
Now loneliness is the only solace I know.

Viable

what can end this endless longing

only a pain like lips to the breast

and the taste of raw skin

drool running down a chest

agony in toes contorted

a body compressed

a sweaty back

a heartbeat distressed

blindness as feeling takes over

begging, a body obsessed

a body of bruises

biology's behest

We Become

in white moonlight we become shadows

with fast breath we become intertwined

I become your lover, you become my love

as you make me an idea, I become a person

your eyes to my eyes, you become a vision

lost in your smile, I become your joy

you become my past as you become my future

in a separate place we become combined

as we reach for each other,

I become me and you become you

Vagabond

I felt the foam of a frangipani.
I lovingly caressed a cactus.
I collected seeds from huayruro.
I rubbed coca leaves on my teeth.
I pressed lupine in a journal.
I wore a string of marigolds like a crown.
I left Icelandic moss to dry on my shelf.

But even after all these years
I never grew anything myself.

Maybe

maybe it's true
maybe your love is this imperfect thing
small and wanting

maybe it isn't your vision
maybe it's better
like fruit from the garden

maybe it isn't all that you wanted
maybe it's much more than you need
like a luxury car

maybe you can't accept this
maybe then it'll be gone
like summer in November

maybe there's someone else out there
maybe there isn't
like the last flight before a snowstorm

maybe you'll regret it
maybe you won't
while you sit on your wrap around porch alone

Summer, I Never Met You

Somehow, I never saw the chicory or
how tall the grass gets or
caterpillars floating in the air.
I missed how rain reshapes the Earth and
where the bugs live and
where hummingbirds die.
All the sunrises and all the sunsets.
And how thick a forest is. And
how quickly they grow.
And the rest of summer
I still don't know.

Consensual

According to doctors
I can't afford to heal.
Slowly
I lay waste to myself.
My body dies
without me.
He will hurt me
again.
My body isn't
mine.
Only my soul.
Who I gave consent
to suffer.

Missing Walls

After seven years, the sweetest,

I carry you away stiff.

No one knows where you're sleeping

and here am I

in a world now strange

and lacking

under a constant battle of

mind and truth

as I walk through

rooms with missing walls.

How long

will I be trapped

in unsound structures

that never collapse

and elude all others.

Insanity

will carry me away

as I carried you

before anyone admits

we are surrounded

by missing walls.

NeFeB

Your body calls me like Neodymium Iron Boron.

I come to your body and there I lay upon.

I open my mouth and taste your perfection until I am full

but now I've tasted enough of your body, give me your soul.

Far Away Friends

I know the way the phone feels pressed against my mouth
and the sound of speaker phone in your car.

I know when you have breaks and what you like to eat
and what time you watch tv and go to sleep.

I know how you look on a phone and in pictures
and the way you sound when you chew.

I know your last six months and what you have planned next
and I know how long you take to respond when you text.

I know what you tell me but that's all.
I don't remember your smell or if your hair is getting long.

I know when you're sad but I don't know how I can hold you.
We can never go out on weekends like other friends do.

I know you left your boyfriend but I never got to meet him.
Just once I want to say, 'see you soon' and mean it.

I know we'll pick up wherever we left off when you call
but I'm forgetting what being near a friend feels like at all.

Guru

Distant songs sing me to sleep
behind a door that never closes
and on the other side of that door: dirty teeth.
My lips are still numb.
I've come to a strange place
where love and death are on the sides of the same street.
As I walk there, what will they call me?
Never teacher.
There are no teachers here, each middle name is teacher.
Then who will listen when I say recycle?
But they do, over and over.
Old ideas that I've come to learn.
The lesson that is never learned
but still, I sit with my back hurting until
they finally pull back the curtain.
I fall through.

Unmet

I let you open my body,
bleed me to death.
I am the lamb until you love me.
After the sacrifice and before
I don't understand the stranger that is myself.
We haven't met.
We are still meeting
until death makes us.
The world wants to name me
but we name ourselves.

How Long it Takes to Change

Spring was always fast
until I finally went outside
and saw only the shadbush and
the Earth still like melting chocolate.
Now spring is as slow as
growing your hair long.

The Quiet Years

Some years are a whisper you barely heard.
A sound you try to remember.
Where did they go and
what did you do and when did they leave?
You wonder until
you live each year a raucous
too loud to sneak.

Elemental Friends

Many friends flow through my life like water.
They come and go but we've both changed when they leave.
I'm left wet and dripping
but they teach me to swim.

A few friendships were born from flame
igniting the passion that burns away old things.
Even the brightest, most beautiful fires die out eventually
leaving me in ashes to begin again.

When friends come through as wind, I briefly know them.
Their sudden force disrupts and imbalances.
I feel them hold me for an instant before vanishing.
I stumble in their wake

but I don't fall. I am on the ground where
my friends of earth hold me steadily.
They are the soil that nourishes me.
We are rocks resting together as the world passes by.

The Good Shepard

Don't be afraid, little lamb,
as the wolves chew off your limbs.
For the Good Shepard stands nearby
watching.
He waits for you.
He has prepared for you
a more perfect body
which you receive once this flesh
has been eaten away.
For your pain
a *great* reward.

Wasteless in Wasteland

This is time,

our gift and coin.

I traded it for sorrow
who hungers endlessly
for time.

Tomorrow,
when I receive time,
I'll trade it for something different;
for all there is left.

But for time,
there isn't much left.

Ships in the Night

Sometimes I see a ship that will take
me back to who I used to be.
It calls me desperately,
offers me promises
seemingly sincere
but I let it
sail away
parting
past.

Small

I met your fears on a mountain.
It was the decay.
It was the passing of time.
It was a stranger in the woods.
How ornate our corpses!
I turned away in disgust.
I was smiling in a sad place though
I was no comfort for its suffering.
We snickered together as schoolgirls.
I miss our secrets as
I find remnants
in old boxes and
around the yard.
They remind me

how small I was on that mountain,
how small I am on this mountain.

More Than

Just behind nature
God sits
with a table set for dinner.
Destitute is still a stranger
I've never met
but plenty
disguises himself
with my wardrobe.

Garden

I've been searching for a garden.
The same one in songs and
on signs, in books and on rooftops,
in movies and out in the backyard.

I finally found that garden.
I've been growing there.
I know joy now
with my feet planted in the soil.
I fall deeper into the earth
as the wind carries my seeds away.

Inward

when I crawl into the mouth of my mother
she swallows me into her womb
the darkness there is full of secrets
she births me once more

when I meet the ghost, I'm quiet
the other ghosts are screaming loud enough
their gifts are curses
and I am cursed

when the trees make conversation
people start to rot and earth plans her funeral
I laugh at everything I've ever done
we die together laughing

when I close my eyes, it isn't dark
there are stars unseen by spaceships
they wait for me as
a dream brings me closer

THE MARRIAGE

An easy escape, I lift from my body.
I leave it to convulse.
I leave it there to cry.
But tonight, there is no exit.
Tonight, our estrangement must die.

We tumble down into the night.
My body and I writhe.
My body and I moan.
We've been here before.
In the fever, we rip off our clothes.

At last, we're left to suffer.
No peace for the discomfort.
No peace for the mind.
A shroud of pain upon the body,
our pasts are now aligned.

Please, another time, another place!
Our very bones, they hurt.
Our bones are made of pain.
We're alone in this darkness.
No use for pleasure, it hurts the same.

A burning mind, a miserable soul.
This agony we must relish.
This agony we must feel.
Our torment we observe,
it's the only way to heal.

No more hiding from what's happened.
We must accept our burden.
We must accept this night.
We must accept the darkness
before we accept the light.

Once we were separate
one part body
one part soul
but now we are united
a person who is whole.

Now You Can Love Me

The only man who loved a girl with caterpillars on her face
died without saying goodbye.

That girl forgot love but learned relationships.

So, she gave and she got but she never was loved.

Until she met herself; they stayed up all night talking and
laughing.

Different

Nothing to share.
Nothing to give.
Why do I breathe?
Why do I live?

So much to share!
So much to give!
That's why I breathe.
That's why I live.

Catalyst

I am not feeble.
Rebellious to circumstance
I rise with the sun.

Celibate

What is kept can be taken.
What is given is not yours.
What may heal may hurt.
What we share is not lost.
What is living is changing.
What is secret is not known.
What is sold is not priceless.
What is gone has vanished.
What has missing parts isn't whole.
What was started can be finished.

What you do with your body
            you do with your soul.

When No One is Watching

she has soft white caterpillars on her face
        she cannot brush them away
                they are lovers
                        destined to furrow

she is a secret too old to be remembered
        her beautiful lips to her beautiful breasts
                she licks and kisses invisible scars
                on her chest

she feels the sadness of a lover who dies last
        she hurts and she cries when she is alone
                her sorrow is desired yet
                      her smiles surprise you

she tried to escape, the gentle flesh won't let her
        she is trapped and saved together
                her body lures you delightfully
                      she touches her round parts

she is gone in the place she made her
        it is quiet there, no one is talking
                all the fingers are simply sewn together
                      she is in the water sleeping
peacefully

Living On a Sphere

Wandering Earth
I end where I began.
The people there sleep safely
believing all is as it once was.
They can't measure where I've been so
now I am only where I am.
But I am no place.
Me is not I and I never came back.

We

all this time *we* were
     and I our impediment
hours exist even now
     when caterpillars crawl over my eyes
        but they already saw
the devil is fond of games
     language, culture, religion, politics
to name a few
     but people make poor playmates

        when the game is over
           we find what we were looking for
            all that there can be
             only *this*

After

when the rivers ran dry

their poison gone

and all the glass in the world

was shattered on the ground

she walked through the chaos

she walked through the crowds

everywhere she looked

every single face that she found

had caterpillars crawling around

Acknowledgements

Thank you, Alex, for always believing in and supporting my
dreams. I would not be where I am today without you.

Thank you
Charles
Lisa
Hanna
Andy
Lauren
Whitney
Anna
Jessica
Libby

About the Author

Uxia Rose is a lifelong writer and creative. She currently resides in Connecticut with her husband and children. Caterpillar Face is her first collection of poetry.

www.ingramcontent.com/pod-product-compliance
Lightning Source LLC
Chambersburg PA
CBHW020742130626
46554CB00006B/2109